T0145017

THE NIGHT BEFORE CHRISTMAS,
THE VERY FIRST ONE

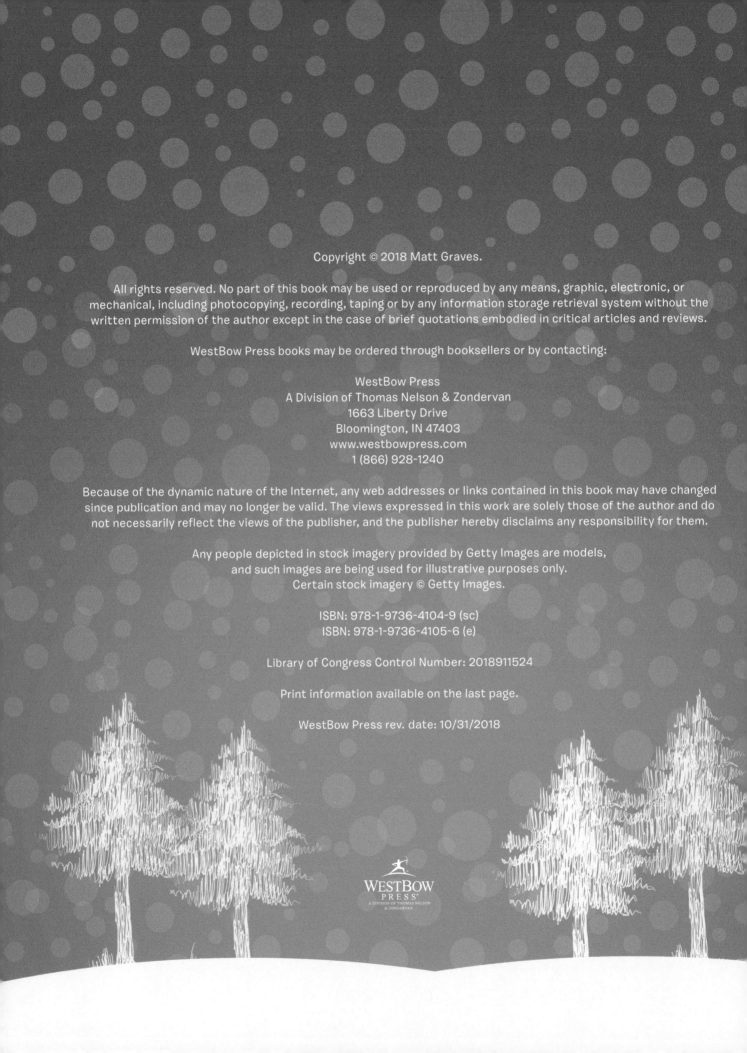

WestBow Press books may be ordered through booksellers or by contacting:

WestBow Press
A Division of Thomas Nelson & Zondervan
1663 Liberty Drive
Bloomington, IN 47403
www.westbowpress.com
1 (866) 928-1240

ISBN: 978-1-9736-4104-9 (sc)
ISBN: 978-1-9736-4105-6 (e)

Library of Congress Control Number: 2018911524

Print information available on the last page.

WestBow Press rev. date: 10/31/2018

WestBow
PRESS®
A DIVISION OF THOMAS NELSON
& ZONDERVAN

THE
NIGHT
BEFORE
CHRISTMAS,
THE VERY FIRST ONE

Matt Graves

'Twas the night before Christmas,
the very first one,
when Mary and Joseph were having a son.
They'd packed up their home
and had left Galilee.
They went to Judea, by Caesar's decree.

They came into town,
and went straight to an inn.
But there were no rooms,
so they could not get in.

They did have a stable,
where they could lie down.
But without a bed,
they slept right on the ground.

The wait was now over,
the time had come near,
to welcome the baby
on that midnight clear.

So Mary gave birth
to a sweet baby boy.
They named the babe Jesus,
He brought so much joy.

See on that great night,
just as God always promised,
He sent down His Son,
to pour blessings upon us.

Somewhere in that region,
out in the dark night,
the shepherds were working,
when they saw a light.

Then, out of nowhere,
did an angel appear.
The shepherds were frozen
and covered in fear.

The angel of God
said, "Do not be afraid.
I bring you good news,
so please hear what I say.
A savior for all has been born on this day.
In the city of David, you'll find him today."

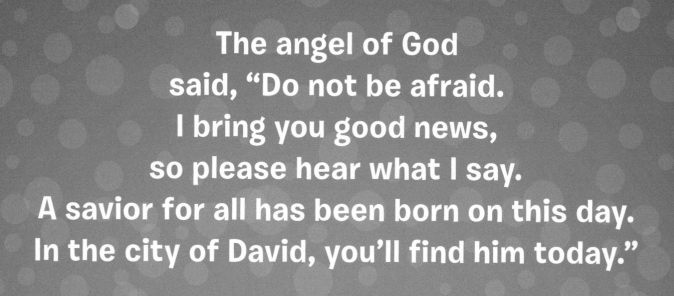

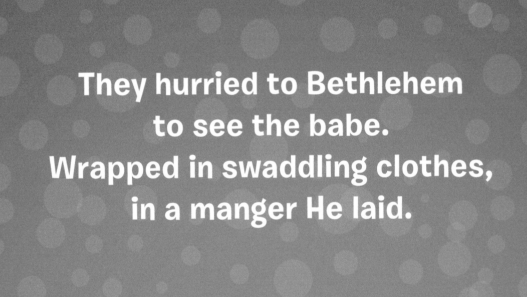

They hurried to Bethlehem
to see the babe.
Wrapped in swaddling clothes,
in a manger He laid.

They glorified God
for what He had just done.
He loved us so much,
He sent Jesus, His Son.

When Jesus grew up,
He did many great deeds.
He taught us to love,
and to help those in need.

He fed those who hungered,
and healed all the lame.

But some were not happy
to hear of His name.

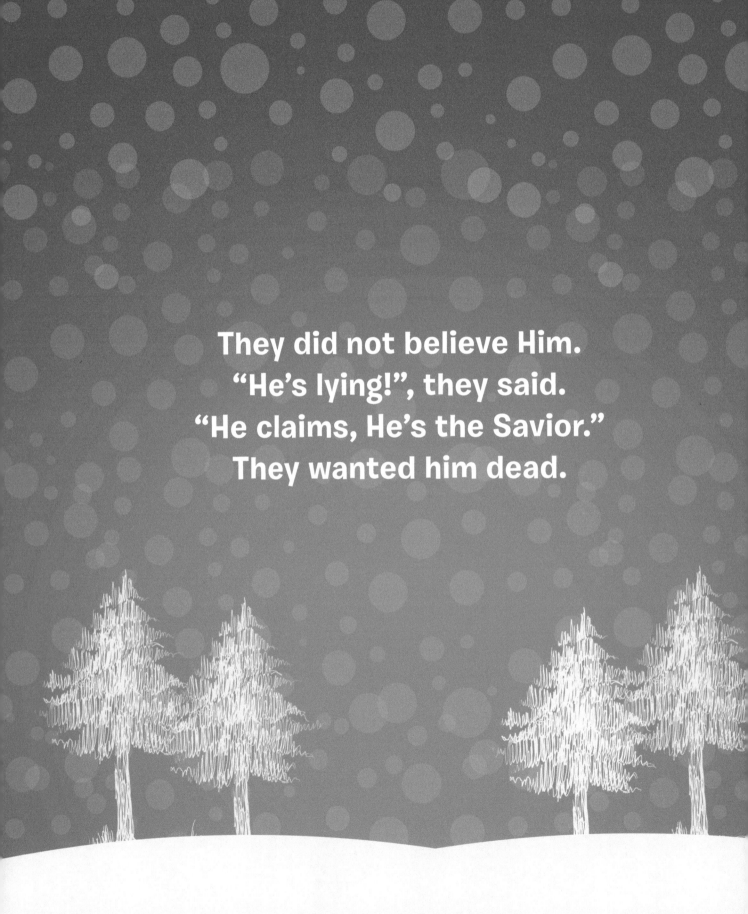

They did not believe Him.
"He's lying!", they said.
"He claims, He's the Savior."
They wanted him dead.

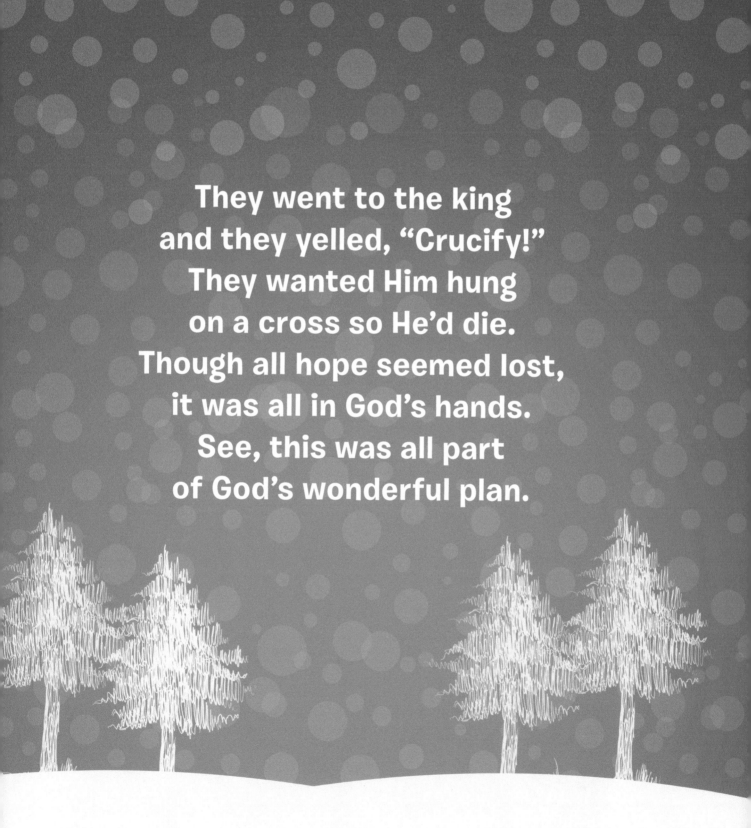

They went to the king
and they yelled, "Crucify!"
They wanted Him hung
on a cross so He'd die.
Though all hope seemed lost,
it was all in God's hands.
See, this was all part
of God's wonderful plan.

So Jesus hung there
on that old rugged cross.
He died for us all
so that we won't be lost.

Then on that third day,
He was raised up again!
To overcome death,
and the power of sin.

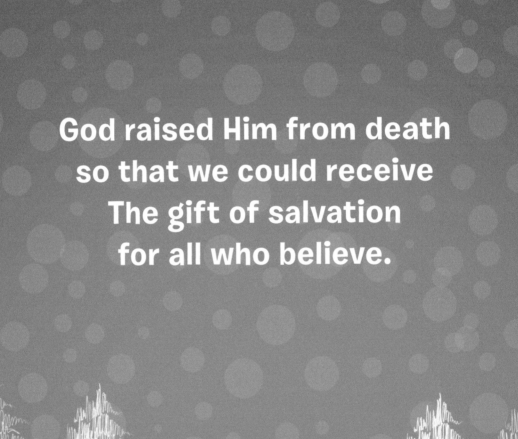

God raised Him from death
so that we could receive
The gift of salvation
for all who believe.

It's neat to think back
how that sweet baby boy,
Came down to this earth
so that we could have JOY.